W9-ART-444

Racism

Gail B. Stewart

KIDHAVEN PRESS™

THOMSON
━━━━━✦━━━━━™
GALE

San Diego • Detroit • New York • San Francisco • Cleveland
New Haven, Conn. • Waterville, Maine • London • Munich

For more information, contact
KidHaven Press
27500 Drake Rd.
Farmington Hills, MI 48331-3535
Or you can visit our Internet site at http://www.gale.com

LIBRARY OF CONGRESS CATALOGING-IN-PUBLICATION DATA

Stewart, Gail B., 1949–
  Racism / by Gail B. Stewart.
    p. cm. — (Understanding issues)
  Includes bibliographical references (p.   ) and index.
  Summary: Defines racism; discusses the history of racism and ways it is being fought today.
    ISBN 0-7377-1025-X
  1. Racism—Juvenile literature. [1. Racism. 2. Prejudices. 3. Race discrimination.
  4. Discrimination.] I. Title. II. Series.
  HT1521 .S67   2003
  305.8—dc21

                                                              2002007606

Printed in the United States of America

Contents

Chapter One

What Is Racism?

Peggy was telling about something that happened the night before. She was upset, and it had to do with her twelve-year-old son, Marc.

"I was driving him home from baseball practice," she said. "We were stopped at a light, waiting for it to turn green. And a boy rides by on a bright orange bike, right by our car. I said to Marc, 'That's a nice bike—I like the color.'"

She stopped talking for a moment, looking bewildered.

"And do you know what my son Marc said?" she asked. "He said, 'Yeah, it's nice. That kid probably stole it.'"

"He's Twelve and He's a Racist!"

She was confused and asked Marc why he thought the bike was stolen. He told her that the boy riding it was black, and he didn't think a black kid could afford a bike that nice.

Peggy was furious. "I told him he had no business making a statement like that," she said. "He

Children learn values from their parents.

didn't know the other boy. He just made an assumption, based on the boy being black. I can't believe it—he's twelve and he's a racist!"[1]

She said that Marc got mad when she said that. He told her that he wasn't a racist, because he doesn't hate black people. He just thought the chances of a boy who was black owning a fancy new bike were pretty slim.

The incident made Peggy both angry and sad. She and her husband thought they had been teaching good values to their children. What had happened? Where did Marc get such ideas?

Making Assumptions

Marc was surprised to be called a racist. He had heard the term many times, and he knew it was a bad thing to be. He thought it has to do with hatred, but it really doesn't. It has to do with making a judgment, or assumption, about someone whom he did not know. A negative judgment made about people before knowing all of the facts is called a **prejudice**.

There are many ways people show prejudice. Sometimes they make assumptions based on sex. Thinking that girls can't play hockey is an example. So is thinking that boys can't be good baby-sitters. Some prejudices are based on age. Is a seventy-year-

People sometimes make quick judgments based on a person's skin color.

old too old to go camping? To take a class in college? People with this prejudice would say so.

Some make assumptions based on a person's job or education. John says he realized he had a prejudice about people who hadn't finished high school.

"I figured someone who dropped out was just a bad student—either lazy or just couldn't do the work," he says. "And then one day my dad told me about my grandfather. When Grandpa Henry was a boy, he quit school in eighth grade, because his father died. Henry went to work in a butcher's shop so his family had money. And my grandfather is probably the smartest guy I know. So I knew it was wrong to assume anything about dropouts."[2]

Racial Prejudice

A lot of prejudices about people are based on **race**. Race is a difficult thing to understand. Centuries ago, some thought that people could be grouped easily into three main categories, or races. The groups were determined mostly by skin color: black (African), white (European), and yellow (Asian). They also believed that the race people belonged to determined their talents and abilities.

However, most scientists believe that the idea of separate races is not true. People cannot be grouped by skin color. Scientists also know that skin color has nothing to do with abilities or talents. Being good at math, being honest, or being good at basketball has nothing to do with what a person looks like.

Skin color does not determine attitude and behavior.

Even so, some people assume things about a person based on the color of his or her skin. That's what Peggy's son Marc did. He believed, without knowing the facts, that a boy who was black could not afford an expensive bicycle. So he assumed that the boy was a thief.

Making the Jump from Thinking to Acting

Racism is a prejudice. It is the belief that people of one race are better or worse than people of another race. For example, some people believe that a black person is not as smart as a white person or a person with brown skin is lazy. Racists are people who think those things. Some racists take action on those thoughts.

Sometimes the action is easy to spot. Oliver and his sister, who are black, were in a gift store. They wanted to buy their mother a present for Mother's Day. They looked at the candles and soaps. They looked at the picture frames and the bracelets. After a few minutes,

Some store clerks watch nonwhite shoppers more closely.

Oliver noticed that the salesperson was following them around. Everytime they turned a corner in the store, the woman stood there watching them.

"I thought she was trying to listen to us talk," says Oliver. "But she wasn't. She just wanted to make sure we weren't stealing things. It made me really mad, too. There were other people in there, but they were all white. That lady wasn't following anybody except us!"[3]

"You Black Kids and Your Babies"

Eleven-year-old Rachel knows what racism is, too. She was carrying her new baby brother around

Being the target of racism is painful and frustrating.

while her parents watched her older brother play soccer. Noah was only eight weeks old, and she loved holding him. As she slowly walked along with the baby, a woman looked at her. She stared at Rachel and Noah. She got a disgusted look on her face.

Says Rachel, "The lady said, 'You black kids and your babies.' She thought I was Noah's mother! I was mad, but I was crying, too. It was embarrassing. My mom told me not to feel bad. She said that the lady had the problem, not me. The lady was racist, because she figured since I was black, I probably had a baby at age eleven. She wouldn't have said that to a white eleven-year-old girl."

Rachel says thinking about that day still makes her feel bad, even though she had done nothing wrong. "I hate that people think bad things about me," she says. "She didn't even know me, and I could just tell that she didn't like me."[4]

A Long History

Thinking that black children are more likely to shoplift, or that young black girls carrying babies must be mothers—these are racist thoughts. But how do people get to be racist? Experts know that it is not a way of thinking that happens overnight.

Unfortunately, the United States has a long history of racism. Knowing about how racism began in this country can help people understand the problem today.

Chapter Two

The Seeds of Racism

Racial prejudice, or racism, is not a new problem in the United States. In fact, some of the very first settlers who arrived from Europe had racist ideas. They saw native people whose skin was dark and whose language was unfamiliar. These people had customs and religions that were unfamiliar, too.

"Kill the Indian, Save the Boy"

The white settlers did not consider the Native Americans to be their equals. In fact, many times they were not thought of as people at all. Settlers called them by disrespectful names, such as "savages" and "redskins." When the settlers wanted more land, they used armies to force the native people far from their homes to live on reservations. That left the best land free for more white settlers.

Some white leaders started a program to teach Native American children in special schools. The children would move away from home and live at the school while they were learning. But what the schools really tried to do was turn native children into white children. The students were not allowed to speak their own language—only English.

"You'd get whipped," says Mary Brown. Her mother attended a school like this when she was very young. "The children were taught to talk like whites, and the teachers gave them new names. Took away their Indian names. Children even had to stop playing Indian games, and learn white games. They had a new religion, too. The teachers had a saying: 'Kill the Indian, Save the Boy.' They thought, 'Get rid of those Indian ways, and underneath is a white boy.'"

Mary says that this thinking did a lot of damage to the Indian people. The children would go home after being away at school for years and they did not

A white teacher instructs Native American students at a school in Pennsylvania in 1903.

remember how to act. "They laughed at their parents," says Mary. "They were white now, inside. And later they just forgot who they really were. They still had brown skin, but they were white. Those teachers taught Indian kids to be racist to their own people."[5]

Anti-Asian Racism

Asians are another group that has faced racism in the United States. Some were Chinese men who came to the United States in the late 1800s. They worked in mines and on farms. They worked long hours in factories. They even helped build the railroads that stretched across the country. But the Chinese often were made to feel unwelcome. Their language and appearance were strange to the Americans. Another reason was that Americans worried that Chinese would get American jobs. Racists struck out against Chinese workers. Many were robbed, beaten, and driven from their homes. Some were even murdered.

Other Asian people experienced racism for different reasons. Japan fought against the United States in World War II. Many Americans worried that Japanese living in the United States were enemies, too. Even Japanese people who had become U.S. citizens were suspected.

In 1942 President Franklin Roosevelt ordered all Japanese people to move to **detention centers** throughout the United States. Government leaders saw this action as a way of protecting the American

A Japanese American man speaks to fellow internees at a relocation camp in Washington State in 1942.

people. The Japanese Americans could take only what they could carry. They had to sell their stores and businesses. Families who had been living in America for many years had become prisoners in their new country.

Racism and Slavery

Black Americans have a very long history as victims of racism. The first black people in the United States did not come voluntarily. They were captured in Africa by traders, and were brought to America in chains. White settlers had large farms and needed lots of laborers to do the hard work. The traders sold Africans to the settlers as slaves. By the end of the eighteenth century, there were almost 4 million African slaves in America.

Slaves toil in a Mississippi cotton field as their owner (foreground) supervises.

The slaves were considered property. To many of the white owners, slaves were not people. They were treated with no more respect than horses or cattle. So it did not matter if an African family stayed together. The husband might be sold to one farmer, and the wife to another. Children were often separated from parents, too.

Like Native Americans, African slaves could not keep their own culture. They had to become Christians instead. They could not speak their native language. They were not allowed to keep their own names, either. Usually the owner let them use his last name, and he picked first names for them. The slaves worked long hours picking crops, weeding, and planting. They received no pay at all. If they tried to escape, they were whipped or killed.

Not all Americans thought slavery was right. Many white people spoke out against it. Even some slave owners freed their slaves after several years. But most slave owners said that slaves should not be freed. They needed to be slaves, said the owners, for black people were not smart enough to live on their own.

Free, but Not Free

The slaves were freed in 1865, after the Civil War. Some people thought that this would end the

Governor George Wallace (second from left) blocks a doorway to prevent the integration of the University of Alabama in 1963.

problems of the black people. But racist thinking was as strong as before. Because of the color of their skin, black people were treated harshly. Southern states, where most of the slave owners lived, passed laws that put limits on black people's new freedom.

For one thing, they were not allowed to vote. They were not allowed to hold jobs other than the most **menial** ones. They could not serve in the army or serve on juries. They could not attend white schools—including state universities. There were racist laws that kept blacks from using public drinking fountains or bathrooms that whites used. There were many other ways that individuals showed their disrespect for black people. Many restaurants had "Whites Only" signs in their windows. In many southern towns, a black person was expected to step off a sidewalk to let any white people nearby have a wider path.

Racism was at the root of a great deal of violence against black people, too. Groups like the **Ku Klux Klan**, dressed in robes and hoods which hid their faces, terrorized black people. Many were beaten and even **lynched** by the racist mobs.

Progress

But there were many people, black and white, who spoke out against such racism. They worked to get rid of racist laws. They worked to change the voting laws and the schools. It took years, but they were successful in changing many things.

Marchers protest police treatment of blacks in McGhee, Arkansas, in 2002.

But while the laws have changed, racism still exists. Many say that racism is as common in the twenty-first century as it ever was. They say that racism still hurts **people of color** in the United States. It may not be as easy to spot as "Whites Only" signs and Ku Klux Klan raids. But its effects are just as destructive.

Chapter Three

Racism in Today's World

O nce most of the obvious signs of racism had disappeared, some Americans felt that the problem had disappeared, too. Unfortunately, racism did not go away.

That often surprises many white people. In a recent survey about racial prejudice, almost 90 percent of whites said they do not have prejudices against people of color. Most also felt that racism was not a big problem in the United States. But blacks and other people of color say that is not so. Racism has not disappeared. Though white Americans do not always notice racism, black Americans notice it all the time.

The Message Is the Same

How can people see racism so differently? One reason is that racists today do not behave the same as they did in 1950 or in 1980. People who are prejudiced against other groups of people are not always angry or mean. A racist person might not even call people names. In fact, many people who have racist ideas can be very polite. But the message they send can be hurtful, too.

Liz, a black high school student, knows that feeling. She was invited to a friend's house a few years ago. What she thought would be a fun afternoon was spoiled.

"Joanne and I were walking in her front door, and her mom is there. And her mom gets this really weird look on her face, like she's just heard bad

Racism can occur in many settings including schools and offices.

news. And I'm thinking, 'She didn't know her daughter's friend was black.' Joanne saw it, too. She tried to rescue the situation. She introduced me to her mom and stuff, but it didn't work.

"Her mom didn't yell or make a scene. She was just cold. She said hello, but I could tell she wanted me gone. It was like she was mad, but she wasn't going to show it until after I left. I'm sure Joanne got yelled at after I left. That was embarrassing for both of us. I don't think she had any idea her mom was going to react that way."[6]

Every Day

Ray, a Native American teen, says that such things happen all the time. "I don't want to say you get used to it," he shrugs. "You don't. It makes you feel bad when people don't like you before they get to know you. But it's a fact of life. It happens every day. After awhile, you just stop being surprised by it."

He says that he and two friends got in an elevator at the mall. A white lady and a baby were already in the elevator. When the three teenagers got in, she bolted out of the elevator.

"We were like, 'What did she think we were going to do to her?'" says Ray. "It was so stupid. She acted like we were murderers or something."[7]

Suspicious

Racism is often a factor in how blacks and other minorities are treated by police, too. Police have been accused of stopping far more blacks on the street than whites.

"You can be walking home from work, and all of a sudden, here comes a cop, lights flashing," says Leo, a black teen. "They want to know why you're out late, what you're doing. I've been stopped so many times I can't count. They've searched my pockets, asked if I'm carrying [a weapon]. Anybody says police aren't looking to arrest black folks, they're wrong."[8]

Many minorities feel police treat them differently from whites.

Black leaders complain that police make assumptions that are unfair. A sure way for a black driver to get stopped, they say, is to drive a shiny new car. Police will assume the car has been stolen. They assume that a black man could not afford such a car.

"My boyfriend has a red Firebird," says one girl. "His mother told him he was going to get stopped every night driving that car. She called it a white man's car. He bought it anyway, but he says his mother was right. One night he picked me up and we went to a party. We got stopped on the way there, and on the way home. He wasn't speeding; he didn't get any tickets. The police just wanted to see his registration!"[9]

Institutional Racism

Blacks and other minorities often face the racist attitudes of individual people. A rude taxi driver may refuse to drive a black passenger. A prejudiced sales clerk may assume black children are shoplifters. But racism also lies behind the actions of entire systems, or institutions.

For example, black children were once banned from white schools. Such **institutional racism** created **segregation**, or the separation of people by race. Segregating black children meant that they had to go to schools that were not as good as white schools. Black schools often had torn and out-of-date textbooks. They did not have nice gyms like white schools did.

Schools in poor neighborhoods often do not receive as much money as schools in wealthy neighborhoods.

But in 1954 the Supreme Court ruled that such segregation was illegal. Black children were entitled to equal education. But that has not happened. The problem is that the school systems get their money from neighborhoods. That means that schools in wealthier neighborhoods are nicer. Because they have more money to spend, they attract better teachers. Inner-city schools, often in run-down neighborhoods, have less money to spend. Their schools are usually run-down, too.

Since white people in the United States tend to live in wealthier neighborhoods than black people, all children do not have the same kind of education. No laws have been broken. But unequal treatment continues.

Redlining

Institutional racism appears in banking, too. Bankers must make decisions about how and where

Some bankers will not loan money to people who live in poor neighborhoods.

they should invest money. They are often asked to help finance new housing. For many years, banks have used a system called **redlining**. The word comes from a red circle bankers draw on the map to remind them where the poorer areas are. Banks consider poor areas to be risky investments.

When someone from one of these redlined areas comes to the bank for a loan, the bank usually does not even consider it. The bank assumes that, based on where the person lives, he or she would not have enough money to repay that loan. On the other hand, someone from an area that is not redlined would be considered. The system is racist, even though the bank is not breaking any law. People of color, who tend to live in poorer neighborhoods, are not treated equally. That means that poorer neighborhoods stay poor. People do not get loans to fix up their homes or to buy new ones.

The Results of Racism

Racism itself is not always easy to spot. Its effects on people are not always obvious, either. But **psychologists**, people who study human behavior, know that there are many effects. One very common result is that people who are treated unfairly become angry and resentful.

Sometimes this anger has turned into violence. In 1991 a black man named Rodney King was beaten by Los Angeles police officers. The police did not know that a passerby saw the beating and

Rioters torched buildings in Los Angeles in 1992 after a jury found police officers not guilty of beating Rodney King.

videotaped it. The police were brought to trial for what they did. However, the jury found the police not guilty.

The nation was shocked. Many black people were angry. Even with a videotape showing King being savagely beaten, they said, a black man could not get justice. The result was four days of rioting in Los Angeles. Fifty people were killed during the violence. Many homes and businesses were burned or destroyed.

"I Don't Feel Proud. I Just Feel Different"

One girl says she tries to ignore kids who laugh about her Native American name. She just smiled

Native Americans experience racism when they are made to feel embarrassed about their heritage.

when someone asked her if she lived in a tepee. But inside, she says, she was angry.

"I was mad at the kids, but—and this sounds bad," she says, looking embarrassed. "But sometimes I feel angrier at my parents than the kids who were mocking me. I felt like, why do we have this stupid last name—why can't we have a normal name? But that's not fair. I know I should be proud of being Ojibwe, and I guess I am. But usually I don't feel proud. I just feel different."[10]

In the Hands of Society

Racism can make people feel ashamed of who they are. A racist society tells certain groups that they are not valued, so eventually, they begin to believe it. Or society tells certain groups that they are not smart enough, or talented enough. After a while, they stop trying. They stop working toward their goals.

When that happens, racism has won. But the cost is very high. And unless society can find a way to fight racism, everyone will lose.

Chapter Four

Fighting Racism

No one has an easy answer for how to get rid of racism. Most people feel that several things have to change before racial prejudice disappears.

The Media

People are influenced by the television shows they watch and the movies they see. But critics say the media have been unfair to minorities. For example, in police dramas, blacks are often shown as drug dealers or gang members. They are shown as violent and dishonest. Whites are usually shown as heroes, who are smart and who obey the law.

By being one-sided, the media is encouraging racism. It strengthens the racist ideas some people already have. Some insist the media need to change. They need to work harder at showing a fair picture of all people.

Education

Many experts believe that education is one of the most important weapons against racism. The

Graduation from high school can lead to more opportunities for success in the future.

opportunities for education have not been equal for black children. Even so, things are beginning to change. More black teens are graduating from high school and going on to college.

Ronnie, eighteen, is going to start college in the fall, and his father, Ken, is proud. "He's the first one in the family to go," says Ken. "My wife finished high school. She was smart enough to go to college, but she didn't have the money. Ronnie is good in math, good in computers. He got a scholarship, and we're getting loans to pay the rest. He's going to do good in college. He'll end up with a good job some day."

Ken says that as more blacks get educated, things will change. "You'll see more people of color buying houses in nicer neighborhoods. Then their kids will be going to better schools. Then pretty soon white people will stop thinking of blacks as welfare bums. You got to change the image, right?"

He laughs. "I've seen some of Ronnie's friends, some of these young black kids. They're sharp. Nobody's going to be accusing them of anything except being successful."[11]

Other Heroes

Schools can help fight racism in other ways, too. For instance, some schools are already taking a new look at what they teach. For many years, English classes did not read books by black authors. There are many great black authors and poets. But because they never studied them, many students did not know it. To them, the only great writers were white.

The same has been true in history classes. In American history, slavery is usually the only time blacks are mentioned. But black patriots made important contributions in the American Revolution. In fact, the very first American to die in the Revolutionary War was Crispus Attucks, a slave. Even so, few children—black or white—had ever heard his name.

Author Maya Angelou recites one of her poems during the 1993 presidential inauguration in Washington, D.C.

Schools are finally beginning to change. They are adding books by black authors to reading lists. History teachers are taking time to focus on the accomplishments of black and Native American people. Getting a more complete picture helps all students understand history better.

Starting with One

Equal education and jobs will help a great deal. However, there is an even better way to get rid of racial prejudice. It does not require laws. It does not require millions of government dollars, either. It can happen within a family. It can happen within one person.

The enemy of racism is information. The more people take the time to learn, the less likely they are to be prejudiced. Sometimes just getting to know someone of another background or skin color can make a difference. Patrick, a twelve-year-old, lives in a wealthy white suburb. He admits he does not really know any black people.

"There are two black kids at my school, but they're not in my grade," he says. "Anyway, I was going to sign up for a basketball clinic, but the one in my neighborhood was full. I got put in a clinic at an inner-city school. It was mostly kids who are black and Native American.

"I was the only white kid, and that was weird at first. No one really talked to me. At first I was wishing I hadn't come, but once the games started, it

By talking and sharing information, young people can learn about other races and cultures.

was fun. By the end, I made friends with four guys, and we decided we'd all sign up for the next clinic together."[12]

Speaking Up

Another thing individuals can do is to speak out the next time someone makes a comment that is racist. All too often people are silent. They do not want to start a fight or cause a scene.

"I never really used to laugh that much when this one friend would tell a joke about black people," says Patrick. "But I never said anything to him, either. Even though I knew it was racist. But after I met [the boys from the basketball clinic] I knew I had to say something.

Individuals must speak out against racism when someone makes inappropriate statements.

By working together, racism may one day become a thing of the past.

"I didn't make a big deal about it. I just said something like, 'Hey, man, come on,' or something. But it worked—he doesn't say stuff like that anymore. At least, around me he doesn't."[13]

Be Proud

Racism is a big problem in the United States. But many Americans are working hard to get rid of racism.

People of different backgrounds and colors are working to bring about change. They want to have a country where people are judged by their actions, not by their skin color. The Pledge of Allegiance contains the words "liberty and justice for all." If more people join the effort, those words will be true someday soon.

Notes

Chapter One: What Is Racism?

1. Personal interview, Peggy, Edina, MN, April 25, 2002.
2. Telephone interview, John, March 16, 2002.
3. Personal interview, Oliver, Minneapolis, MN, April 3, 2002.
4. Telephone interview, Rachel, May 1, 2002.

Chapter Two: The Seeds of Racism

5. Personal interview, Mary, Minneapolis, MN, August 12–15, 1996.

Chapter Three: Racism in Today's World

6. Telephone interview, Liz, April 22, 2002.
7. Personal interview, Ray, Minneapolis, MN, June 12, 1997.
8. Personal interview, Leo, Minneapolis, MN, May 7, 2002.
9. Personal interview, name withheld, May 2, 2002.
10. Personal interview, Jane, St. Paul, MN, November 1998.

Chapter Four: Fighting Racism

11. Personal interview, Ken, Richfield, MN, February 2000.
12. Telephone interview, Patrick, April 2, 2002.
13. Patrick, interview.

Glossary

detention centers: Special holding areas for Japanese people in the United States during World War II. Japanese people who lived on the West Coast were moved to the camps so that they could not aid the Japanese army.

institutional racism: Policies or practices of systems such as education, banking, and so on that result in the unequal treatment of people.

Ku Klux Klan: A hate group targeting black people and other minorities. The Klan originated in the South after the Civil War and was responsible for many beatings and deaths.

lynch: To hang someone without a trial.

menial: The kind of work done by a servant. Such work often pays little.

people of color: Usually refers to people who are not white.

prejudice: An opinion formed without regard to facts.

psychologists: People who study human behavior.

race: A group of people who share similar physical characteristics. Scientists once believed that it was possible to sort people into three races; today, most scientists say that is not possible.

racism: The belief that skin color determines a person's intelligence, honesty, or other characteristics.

redlining: A system banks have sometimes used to decide which neighborhoods are bad risks for loans.

segregation: The separation of people based on their race.

For Further Exploration

Books

Ellen Levine, *Freedom's Children: Young Civil Rights Activists Tell Their Own Stories.* New York: Puffin, 2000. Very readable, with good emphasis on what individuals can do to stop racism.

Rita Milios, *Working Together Against Racism.* New York: Rosen, 1995. Good information on racist hate groups throughout history.

Angela Phillips, *Discrimination.* New York: New Discovery, 1993. Though somewhat dated, this book has an excellent section on injustice to Native Americans as well as a helpful glossary.

Cath Senker, *Why Are People Prejudiced?* Austin, TX: Raintree Steck-Vaughn, 2002. Good background on the history of racism and other types of prejudice.

Nasoan Sheftel-Gomes, *Everything You Need to Know About Racism.* New York: Rosen, 1998. Somewhat more difficult reading, but suitable for advanced readers. Good list of places to contact for more information.

Gail Stewart, *The Other America: The Elderly.* San Diego: Lucent Books, 1996. Contains interviews with a Japanese man who was sent to a detention camp during World War II, and with an elderly black man who has seen changes in black-white relations over his lifetime.

Index

Picture Credits

About the Author

Gail B. Stewart has written over ninety books for young people, including a series for Lucent Books called The Other America. She has written many books on historical topics such as World War I and the Warsaw ghetto.

Stewart received her undergraduate degree from Gustavus Adlophus College in St. Peter, Minnesota. She did her graduate work in English, linguistics, and curriculum study at the College of St. Thomas and the University of Minnesota. She taught English and reading for more than ten years. Stewart and her husband live in Minneapolis with their three sons.